Youth Master of Business Administration Series

Business Law

A learning workbook program for junior high and high school students.

Visit the Y.M.B.A. website at www.YMBAgroup.com

ISBN-13: 978-1725514607
ISBN-10: 1725514605

Printed by CreateSpace, An Amazon.com Company.
Available from Amazon.com and other retail outlets.
CreateSpace, Charleston, SC

Copyright protected © 2015, 2018, 2020
All rights reserved.
This workbook publication, or any part of this book, may not be reproduced, distributed, stored in a
retrieval system, or transmitted in any form for any purpose without prior written approval from the autho

Consult a professional when seeking business advice and decisions. This is a learning book discussing
topics in a general style, not intended to be considered professional advice, suggestions, or guidance.

Submit all inquiries at the website www.YMBAgroup.com

Y.M.B.A. Business Law - grades 6 7 8 9 10 +   ages 12 13 14 15 16 +

Business Law

We hope to hear from you!

Suggestions, Ideas, Questions
always welcome at
www.YMBAgroup.com

THE Y.M.B.A. GROUP - BUSINESS LAW
Business Law, Contracts and Cases

TABLE OF CONTENTS

How To Use This Learning Workbook	7
What Is Business Law	8
Government Structure and Documents	10
Inside The Courtroom	18
Legal Documents - Content and Layout	22
Appeals	24
Legal Terms	26
Contracts	32
Contract Enforcement	36
Individual and Property Torts	40
Trial Procedures	44
The Jury	48
Supreme Court Cases	50
Business Law Review Quiz	62
Answer Key	68
Completion Certificate	71

Do you have a suggestion for a book topic?

Let us know! It may be our next workbook!

www.YMBAgroup.com

How To Use This Book

Thank you for choosing the Y.M.B.A. learning workbook series. I am excited to share the topics with you. As a teacher, corporate professional, M.B.A. and parent, I sought to find a quality program for my children that was both at an introductory level and interesting for their age. When I discovered nothing like this existed, Y.M.B.A. began. A business learning program for young students created and designed by an M.B.A, teacher, and parent. Y.M.B.A. presents information in clear, easy to follow style; focused on students approximately 12 to 16 years of age. I designed the lessons as a combination textbook and workbook because students retain far more when applying the newly taught ideas. The series instructs one idea at a time in a clear and simple to understand format. While presenting students with a concept they develop their understanding with fun, level-appropriate examples. After each lesson page is a worksheet to apply the idea from the page prior. This pattern keeps students engaged and actively learning by seeking on-going student applications. The "The Drawing Board" worksheets reinforce the lesson as students practice reasoning, computation, or analysis. The Y.M.B.A. focuses on useful business concepts and everyday topics found across industries and in daily life.

Each learning workbook has a quiz for a student demonstration of their new understanding of the subject. You will likely see an increase in both pride and confidence as the student completes the learning workbook. Why wait for business concepts to be introduced? Students are ready to learn about practical life and business topics today. Y.M.B.A. lessons include relevant examples based on familiar student scenarios to sustain learning that is both effective and fun!

Business skills are utilized in every industry; an understanding of business is essential. Why wait? Students can begin achieving more with Y.M.B.A. today and build a path for the future. Your support is appreciated. Suggestions, questions, or comments are always welcome.

Thank you,

L.J. Keller

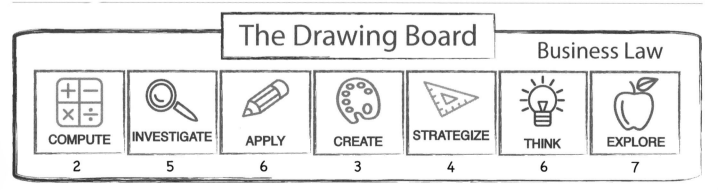

The quantity of each skill practice area is shown below each learning tile.
Worksheet pages seek to capture student interest and build learning momentum.

What Is Business Law?

The goal of the law is to provide a fair and balanced way to settle disputes. The court system works to to oversee disputes impartially. To help maintain a fair system, the local, state, and national government has laws and procedures that people follow when wanting the court's assistance in a solution to a conflict. A court will help make sure that each side of the disagreement is treated fairly, and that those involved are participating legally, as they seek to settle the matter.

To better understand business law topics, an understanding of law as it relates to your everyday life is helpful. Understanding the law and the legal system can help you in the future and may even possibly help avoid a legal dispute. If you find your business in a legal dispute, a basic legal knowledge will help you understand the court process. The decision of a judge on a legal matter is known as a **ruling**. A ruling in court can be helpful in future court cases. A court of law may have previously decided on a legal matter similar to a scenario you encounter. You may refer to a prior court ruling is helpful to to understand the law better as it relates to your case matter (situation). The earlier court case ruling being referred to is known as **precedent**. Precedent is when a judge's decision on a different court case helps understand the law as it relates to current personal or business legal scenarios.

The most common people involved in the legal process are known as lawyers (attorneys) and judges. A lawyer will attend three years of college after earning a four-year college degree. A judge is most often a lawyer before becoming a judge of the court.

The two sides that disagree in a legal dispute may be a:

Person v. Person	Person v. Business	State v. Person
Person v. Group of People	Business v. Group of People	State v. Business
Group of People v. Group of People	Business v. Person	Business v. State

v = Verses
Plaintiff v. Defendant

Careers In Business Law:

- Lawyer
- Judge
- Court Reporter
- Legal Analyst
- Courtroom Security
- Legal Interpreter
- Legal Human Resources
- Court Clerk
- Computer Technology

The Drawing Board

Listed below are two columns. Column one has facts about various plaintiff details. Column two has details about possible defendants. Draw a line to connect the plaintiff with the likely defendant.

Plaintiff   Defendant

November 7, 2:00 pm
Car dented in the parking lot.
Purple paint seen on the white car.

November 7, 1:50 pm
Parking lot video camera shows a purple car speeding from the parking lot.

July 12, 4:15 pm
Wallet taken from a bag at the bank.

April 10, 1:00 pm
Defendant emails a picture with the bicycle outside the library.

April 10, 1:30 pm
Bicycle not on the bike rack at the library. Bicycle placed on rack at 12:45 pm.

October 25, 2:30 pm
Defendant is pulled over for speeding, and the officer notices a package without an address label.

June 12, 11 am
Phone dropped out of pocket between 5th and 6th street.

February 9, 1:50 pm
Defendant is seen throwing mail with the plaintiff's address in the trash.

February 9, 11:45 am
Mail delivered by the post office.

July 12, 4:25 pm
Defendant calls friend, says just picked up $40 at the bank.

October 25, 2:30 pm
Package left at the front door.
Postage label found, no package.

June 12, 1 pm
Phone calls are made to the defendant's mom, friend, and school.

May 18, 9:15 am
Employee leaves to go to the bank to make a company deposit, $512.

August 30, 1:45 am
Defendant is on the security video and sets off the alarm from inside.

August 29, 10:15 pm
Manager locks the store for the night and turns on the alarm.

January 24, 9:00 am
First customer of the store buys one shirt and one ring is missing.

January 24, 8:55 am
One employee opens the store, sets up a new ring display at the counter.

May 18, 9:40 am
The defendant who works at the same company deposits $500 to their personal bank account.

INVESTIGATE

Copyright Protected.   www.YMBAgroup.com

Government Structure

The government of the United States is divided into three departments. The departments are also known as branches of government. The three branches work together with the common goal of helping the country. The idea for the three branches of government is included in the United States Constitution.

The laws and legal procedures followed in the United States are based on ideas from many different groups over thousands of years. The founding fathers who created the Constitution of the United States looked to history for ideas. The ideas for many of the laws come from the Roman Empire. Specific rules, and the penalty for breaking the law, in the United States today are similar to laws in ancient Rome. The United States Constitution also includes ideas about property ownership based on concepts from England. But not all laws were written into the Constitution in the 1700s. Founding Fathers of the United States Constitution were aware that the country, and the people, would change. The Constitution allows for changes called *amendments*, so that the document can be effective in any period. The document provides for changes to current laws and rights and even the addition of entirely new ideas. The Founding Fathers saw that in history a conflict began when a document or law did not change with the people. A contract that was too rigid (strict) and did not work well. A document that does not change can become outdated or ignored. The United States Constitution was created to allow for changes to meet the needs and wants of the citizens.

Legislative Branch
Senate and House of Representatives
Talks With Citizens About Possible Laws
Writes The Laws
Sends The President Possible New Laws
Elected By Citizens

Executive Branch
The President
Reviews The Possible New Laws
Signs To Approve A Law
Will Veto A Law To Make It Not Approved
Elected By Citizens

Judicial System
Judges and The Courts
Judges The Laws For Fairness
Decides If Laws Are Used Correctly
Selected By The President

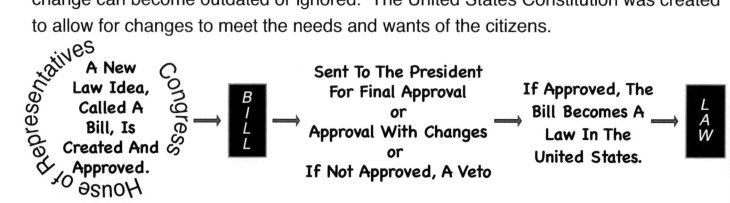

The Drawing Board

Imagine you are the legislative branch of your home. Create new laws to help manage the day to day activities where you live. Create four possible laws for consideration by the Home President (also known as a parent or guardian). Present the laws to your 'President" for approval, approval with changes, or a veto. Remember, a law is in place to protect the rights of all people.

First Proposed Law:

The new law will be helpful by:

★ ★ ★ ★ ★ ★ ★

Executive Branch - Circle A Decision

Approved

Approved With Changes

Veto

Second Proposed Law:

The new law will be helpful by:

★ ★ ★ ★ ★ ★ ★

Executive Branch - Circle A Decision

Approved

Approved With Changes

Veto

Third Proposed Law:

The new law will be helpful by:

★ ★ ★ ★ ★ ★ ★

Executive Branch - Circle A Decision

Approved

Approved With Changes

Veto

Fourth Proposed Law:

The new law will be helpful by:

★ ★ ★ ★ ★ ★ ★

Executive Branch - Circle A Decision

Approved

Approved With Changes

Veto

CREATE

Copyright Protected.   www.YMBAgroup.com

Local, State and Federal Governments

Local Courts

A local court is responsible for enforcing the laws put in place by the local town. For example, an incorporated village may have metered car parking. If a person is breaking the law of the village by not paying for the parking, the town may issue a ticket. The person who received the ticket would have a choice to pay the ticket or attend a court date at the local court to explain why the ticket should not be paid. The local court judge will rule (decide) on the request.

> The Founding Fathers were concerned that the United States may one day have a leader who acted like a king. The people that founded the United States lived under the rule of the King of England for many years. The people of the newly formed country of the United States saw how the leadership of a king led to the freedoms of only *some* citizens as being important. The people in the United States wanted to be sure the rights of the people were more important than the power of a king. The freedoms given to United States citizens are one of the reasons immigrants came from around the world to the United States. Freedom gives citizens the chance to find happiness and success.

State Courts

A state court is responsible for enforcing laws established by the state government. For example, if a company is found not to be disposing of chemicals using the methods required by the state, a ticket or violation may be issued to the company. The company representative, or owner, would have the choice to pay the fine and follow the law, or to attend a hearing at the courthouse to explain why the law should not apply to the company.

> Freedom is a foundation of the government in the United States. The Constitution details the rights of citizens and any right not specifically given to the Federal Government is a right kept by the states and citizens.

Federal Courts

A federal court is responsible for enforcing laws established by the federal (national) government. Any disagreement between states is settled by the federal government. Imagine if one state claimed an island off the coastline as belonging to the state. But, the neighboring state believed the island belonged to their state. A federal court judge would oversee the legal court case as the two sides present details about why the island belongs to their state.

The Drawing Board

When a person violates the law the issue may be overseen by a local, state, or federal court. Consider each of the legal situations below. Write an L if a local court will consider the facts. Write an S if a state court will decide the case. Write an F if a federal court will consider the evidence.

L = Local Court   S = State Court   F = Federal Court

_____ 1. A car is parked on the street in the space marked, "Mayor Only".

_____ 2. Driving a car too fast on a highway.

_____ 3. A national USA company double-charged 1,000,000 customers for their electric on last years invoices.

_____ 4. A business truck weighs more than the allowed limit on a highway.

_____ 5. Large trash is unloaded from a truck and placed on the side of a residential street in a non-trash area.

_____ 6. The national government passes a new law. A national company does not believe it should apply toward their business.

_____ 7. A person is ticketed for not wearing shoes in a public park.

_____ 8. Two states disagree about how to share toll-road money collected on a shared bridge that allows travelers to drive between states.

THINK

Copyright Protected.   13   www.YMBAgroup.com

United States Constitution

After the United States won independence from England, a document called The Articles of Confederation was used as the laws for the country. Soon after the leaders of the new government decided that the Articles of Confederation did not cover all the ideas needed for the new and developing United States. A group of men known as the Founding Fathers wrote the document that would be the foundation of laws and freedoms in the United States.

The United States Constitution

The first paragraph in the Constitution is called the *preamble*. The preamble is the introduction to the document and explains that the main goal is to establish a peaceful and fair country so current and future citizens are free to pursue happiness. The document is then divided into sections called *articles*.

Article I
The Legislative Branch: Congress & The House of Representatives

Article II
The President

Article III
The Judicial System

Article IV
The States

Article V
How To Add Amendments (Changes)

Article VI
Following The Rules Of The Constitution

Article VII
At Least 9 States Needed To Ratify (Approve) The Constitution

What is an **amendment**?

An amendment is a change to a current idea, or the adding of a totally new idea, to the Constitution. There are a total of 27 amendments to the United States Constitution that have been approved by the legislative, executive, and judicial branches of government and the citizens.

The Drawing Board

The United States Constitution presents ideas, guidelines and laws for the citizens of the country. Each citizen in the United States has freedoms and rights guaranteed by the Founding Fathers in the Constitution. Each citizen is expected to follow the law.

Following instructions is necessary to understand the legal documents of a society. Follow the clues below to practice following instructions to solve the puzzle.

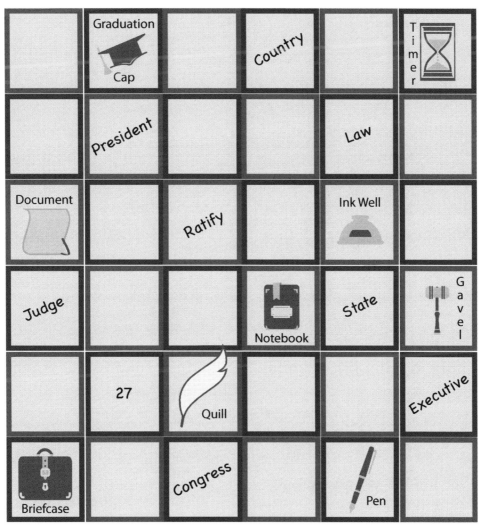

You are on the top row, left-most box. You move three spaces right to land in the _____ box. You move down one, and to the right one to the _____ box. From there you move to the box in the same column that has two of the same letters in its name. From there you move left four boxes to the box with the word _____. Now move diagonally up three boxes to the _____ box and back two boxes.

You are done! The final box is the _____.

Constitutional Amendments

A simple overview of the amendments to the United States Constitution.

The Bill of Rights = First 10 Amendments

#	Year	Details
1	1791	Freedom of speech, writings, meetings, and petitions.
2	1791	Organized people seeking to defend freedoms and citizens have the right to bear arms and weapons.
3	1791	Soldiers must have homeowner permission to enter a home.
4	1791	Good reasons need to be known before a government or police can arrest, or search a person and their property. The requirement of a good reason to search is known as *probable cause*.
5	1791	A person can only be put on trial in a court one time per crime. Not being on trial more than once for the same crime is known as *double-jeopardy*.
6	1791	Trials will begin quickly after charges are filed against a person. The accused person will be aware of the legal charges and have a fair trial.
7	1791	All non-criminal court cases (disputes) will have a jury to decide the case.
8	1791	Bail will be reasonable amounts; punishments will not be cruel or unusual.
9	1791	People have more rights than listed in the Constitution and Bill of Rights.
10	1791	States and its people decide any items not covered in the Constitution.

17 Additional Amendments Passed By Congress & Approved By The States

#	Year	Details
11	1795	A state in the United States may not be sued by a citizen.
12	1804	Details on how to manage the election process.
13	1865	Slavery is illegal nationwide in the United States.
14	1868	People born in the United States are citizens.
15	1870	The right to vote belongs to all male citizens who follow the law.
16	1913	The national federal government may tax a citizens income.
17	1913	Citizens, not appointed by legislatures, will elect senators.
18	1919	Prohibition begins, drinking alcohol is illegal in the United States.
19	1920	Women may vote. All citizens who follow the law may vote.
20	1933	Details on the work dates for Congress and the President.
21	1933	Prohibition ends, drinking alcohol is legal in the United States.
22	1951	Presidents can not be elected for more than two terms.
23	1961	Citizens in Washington, D.C. can now vote for President.
24	1964	Taxes can not be charged to earn the right to vote.
25	1967	Explains who leads the country after the President or Vice-President.
26	1971	Citizens starting at age 18 can vote, lowered from 21 years of age.
27	1992	Salary limit amounts set for members of Congress.

The Drawing Board

Consider the following questions about Constitutional amendments.

1. The Bill of Rights is the first ten amendments to the Constitution. The Bill of Rights was added to the Constitution in 1791. Which of the ten Bill of Rights amendments do you feel are most important? Why?

2. Which of the ten Bill of Rights amendments to the Constitution do you feel is the best example of what makes the United States different from other governments? Explain your answer using an example.

3. Sending an email on the computer is not mentioned explicitly in the Bill of Rights. Do the rights of citizens include emails? How is it that citizens can have rights in an email even though computers were not yet invented when the document was written?

4. Since the Bill of Rights 17 amendments have been added to the Constitution. Which of these 17 amendments do you think should have been passed into law sooner than when it actually became a law?

5. Imagine you are a member of Congress. Your job is to create the 28th amendment to the United States Constitution. What is your amendment?

EXPLORE

Inside The Courtroom

Layout and Function

Each courtroom in the United States has a very similar layout. The layout of a room is the overall design and where important parts of the design are located. Consider the floor plan below of a basic courtroom.

Notice one side of the room is the defendant, the defense lawyer, and an area for people to watch the courtroom events while support is given to the defendant. On the opposite side of the courtroom is the plaintiff, the plaintiff attorney, and an area for people who support the plaintiff. These are the common locations in the courtroom to find key people during the court activities. Each courtroom will also have the judge sitting close to the center of the room. A witness stand will be located in the room, often it is close to the jury seating area. There is also a specific area in the courtroom for the stenographer and the bailiff. By keeping a similar layout in the courtroom, lawyers, and all those involved in the case, can know what to expect in the courtroom. Each side can focus their attention on preparing and presenting the best case to the judge.

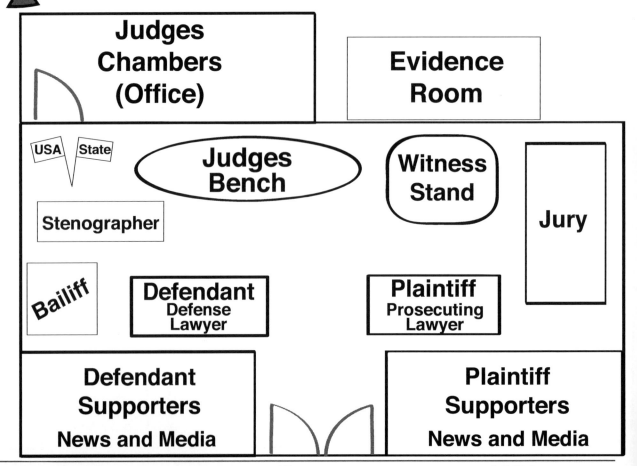

The Drawing Board

Review the courtroom layout on the previous page. Next, read the clues below describing a person found in the courtroom. Match the letter from the court layout below to the member of the court that is described.

_____ 1. Local citizens who listen to the details to decide guilty or innocent.
_____ 2. The place where items from the case are kept until shown in court.
_____ 3. The person or company accused of a crime.
_____ 4. An attorney working with the person or company who was hurt.
_____ 5. The news and media businesses that will report the story to the public.
_____ 6. The person or company who claims the defendant hurt them.
_____ 7. The person who keeps a record of activity in the courtroom.
_____ 8. Friends and family of the person accused of a crime.
_____ 9. The security or police officer in the court.
_____ 10. The person who oversees the courtroom and decides a punishment.
_____ 11. Friends and family of the side claiming harm by the defendant.
_____ 12. A person who saw, or has details, to help understand the case.
_____ 13. An attorney working with the person, or company, accused of a crime.

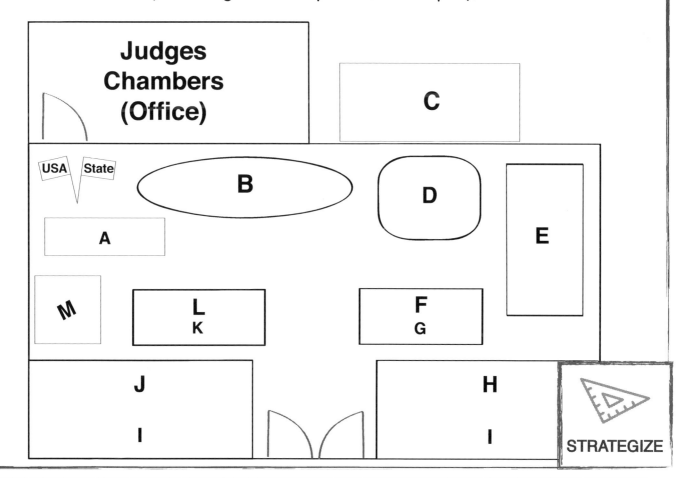

STRATEGIZE

People Of The Court

There are many different jobs that people enjoy each day in a court of law. There are also people involved with a court case that are not employees of the court. For example, the witness for a trial and the people that come to watch the court events, are not employees of the court. The people involved in a legal case have a specific job and purpose during a court case with the common goal of a fair trial.

Judge - The person who is in charge of the court. When there is no jury in a case, the judge will make a decision of innocent or guilty and decide the punishment in the case.

Stenographer - The person who writes, types, or organizes the details of the legal case, so the case details can be recorded in a document.

Bailiff - The person who maintains a police or security presence in the court.

Defendant - The person or business charged with a crime and is hopeful to present a defense in an effort to not pay a fine or go to jail.

Defendant Supporters - People most commonly family and friends of the defendant.

Defendant Lawyer - The person who speaks on behalf of the accused defendant.

Witness - The person who saw, heard or has items that are useful to either the plaintiff or defendant in the court case.

Plaintiff - The person or business who states the defendant did something wrong or against the law and requests the court to judge the person as guilty.

Plaintiff Supporters - People who are most often family and friends of the plaintiff.

Plaintiff Lawyer - The person who speaks on behalf of the plaintiff.

Jury - The group of people who will decide if the defendant is guilty or innocent in a civil or a criminal legal case in a courtroom.

Copyright Protected.   www.YMBAgroup.com

The Drawing Board

Oops! Your legal terms dictionary fell off the desk. The words and their meanings are all mixed up! Cross out the word or words that are incorrect in the definitions below. Next, write the corrected word that should be in the place of the incorrect word.

1. Judge - The person who is in charge of the courtroom. The judge will make a decision of innocent or guilty and decide the dinner after a case.

2. Stenographer - The person who writes, types or organizes the details of the lunchroom so the case details are recorded.

3. Bailiff - The person who maintains a police or security presence in the court park.

4. Defendant - The person or business charged with a misdemeanor or felony and is defending themselves in the hope of not being found sleeping.

5. Defendant Supporters - People, most commonly family and friends, of the mayor.

6. Defendant Lawyer - The person who speaks on behalf of the accused plant.

7. Witness - The person who saw, heard, or has items that are useful to either the plaintiff or defendant during the vacation.

8. Plaintiff - The person or business who says the defendant did something wrong or against the law and requests legal helicopters.

9. Plaintiff Supporters - People, most often family and friends, of the jury.

10. Plaintiff Lawyer - The person who presents the gift on behalf of the plaintiff.

11. Jury - The lawyer who will decide if the defendant is guilty or innocent during a legal dispute in a painting of law.

INVESTIGATE

The Documents

Complaint - The complaint document will tell the court and the defendant why the plaintiff has started a lawsuit. The complaint will include the details of why the plaintiff feels harmed and what the plaintiff wants from the defendant.

Motion To Dismiss - A request that is made to the court to have the legal dispute ended. The plaintiff or the defendant can tell the judge that there is not enough admissible (allowed) evidence to continue the lawsuit. The judge will examine the evidence and case details to decide if the lawsuit will be dismissed or allowed to continue.

Judgment - The final written decision in a lawsuit from a judge. The judgment is the final decision. A judgment will include what is expected from both the plaintiff and the defendant in the court case.

STATE OF FLORIDA
UNITED STATES OF AMERICA - FLORIDA ORANGE COUNTY COURT

County Case Docket Number: 15-CL5467

Jump Aroopo Bounce House Rentals, Inc.,
Plaintiff

vs.

COMPLAINT

Bounce Manufacturing Company
Defendant

Date: May 10, 2018

1   Facts
2 On January 8, 2018, seven water splash bounce houses were delivered to
3 the Plaintiff. The product model number 477 is listed in the Defendant
4 company catalog as 12 feet tall. Upon arrival, the Plaintiff set up each
5 bounce house to ensure proper inflation. One bounce house failed to inflate
6 and did not blow up to take shape. All seven bounce houses measured eight
7 feet tall at the highest point. The Plaintiff contacted the Defendant to return
8 the seven bounce houses. The Defendant stated returns would not be accepted.
9
10   Conclusion
11 The Plaintiff requests the court grant a full refund for the cost of the seven
12 bounce houses. The bounce houses delivered were not as advertised. Also,
13 the one bounce house is defective and does not blow up to inflate. The Plaintiff
14 also requests the Defendant be responsible for the cost of the return shipping.
15 The Plaintiff requests the Defendant pay the costs of attorney fees.
16
17
18   C.A. Page
19   Attorney for Plaintiff
20   28 Valley Park Drive
21   Winter Park, Florida 32457

The Drawing Board

Imagine you are the judge. Consider the complaint document on the previous page. During the court case you saw evidence to show:

(1) The catalog for Bounce Manufacturing said the inflatable model number 477 would be 12 feet tall. (2) The Bounce Manufacturing Company policy says all non-working items will be refunded. (3) The Bounce Manufacturing Company invoice says all items that inflate at delivery will not be accepted as a return and the company will not give the customer a refund.

STATE OF FLORIDA
UNITED STATES OF AMERICA - FLORIDA ORANGE COUNTY COURT

County Case Docket Number: 15-CL5467

Jump Aroopo Bounce House Rentals, Inc.,
Plaintiff

vs.

Bounce Manufacturing Company
Defendant

JUDGMENT

Date: May 27, 2018

JUDGES SUMMARY OF FACTS

1
2
3
4
5
6
7
8
9
10   JUDGES DECISION
11
12
13
14
15
16   _____
                                        your signature
17
18
19   _____
            your name
20   Orange County Court Judge
            1776 Federal Court
21   Orlando, Florida 32802

CREATE

Copyright Protected.   23   www.YMBAgroup.com

Appeals

What is an **appeal**?

When a court decides a case sometimes a defendant (in criminal cases) or a plaintiff or a defendant (in non-criminal cases) can ask for another trial. An appeal is a request to a court to review the details of a decision made by a judge based on the case details. The person who asks for an appeal wants a judge to review the details and declare in writing that the decision in the original case was unfair or incorrect.

The person or business asking for an appeal is known as an *appellant*.

If an appeal is not agreed to by the appeals court, the appellant has one last option. The appellant may submit a request for the Supreme Court of the United States to give a new court trial. If granted, the Plaintiff and Defendant from the original court case will participate in the new court case at the Supreme Court of the United States.

The United States Supreme Court has 9 Judges Who Decide Cases.

The Supreme Court of the United States is the highest court in the country. The decision of the Supreme Court Judges is the final decision on any court case. The Supreme Court considers each case and makes decisions based on the facts of the case and if they are in agreement with (or in violation of) current laws. Supreme Court decisions can be used as information in future court cases.

In a civil case either side may appeal a judges decision.

In a criminal case only the defendant may appeal the judge's decision.

Why does the law give a defendant permission to appeal a decision in a criminal case?

Are the appeal rules fair to all citizens in the country? Why or why not?

THINK

Copyright Protected.   24   www.YMBAgroup.com

The Drawing Board

When an attorney files a request for an appeal it is requested at an appellate court. An appeal is a request to the court after one trial to have permission for a second trial in the hope of a different result. Certain reasons are allowable when requesting an appeal. Simply not being happy with the result of the first court case is not an appeals reason.

Acceptable appeal requests include:
(a) a belief that evidence in the case was changed or not accurate
(b) a belief that a jury member was offered money for their decision
(c) new evidence that is highly reliable and shows the guilty person as not guilty
(d) any other reason about a large error in the original court case

Consider the reasons of the appeal below.
If a reason is acceptable for an appeal, circle the item.
If an item is not reasonable for an appeal, strike through the item with a line.

1. A defendant is found guilty, but scientific evidence just tested shows it to be impossible to have been the defendant.

2. The evidence clerk in the judge's courtroom of the defendant who was judged to be guilty attended the same college as the plaintiff.

3. A juror on the case was just convicted of accepting money from the plaintiffs family member.

4. A defendants parent feels her child is sorry and should be able to come home for the holiday.

5. The defendant believes the attorney was not responsible in their job and should have worn a blue suit on court dates.

6. A defendant testified (spoke) as a witness during the trail and would like to have smiled more at the jury while answering some questions.

7. The defendant is charged with a crime at 11:00 am in Atlanta, GA. The defendant is found guilty, although they claim they were in Los Angeles, CA when the crime happened. The local toll-booth company in California has discovered pictures from the day that show the defendant in Los Angeles at the time of the crime.

APPLY

Legal Terms

ACQUITTAL - When a person charged with a crime is found not guilty by a court. *Henry was excited at the news of his brother's acquittal.*

ANSWER - The reply written by the defendant, or their attorney, to a court matter.

CEASE AND DESIST - An order for a person or business to immediately stop doing an act, either permanently, or while waiting for the results of a court case.

CONTEMPT OF COURT - Actions by a person who ignores a judges order.

EVIDENCE - Presented by the plaintiff or defendant in a trial to support their claims in court. Evidence may be spoken, written, photographic, recorded, or scientific.

EXPERT WITNESS - A person who is a professional in a specific field of study and often has both a formal educational background and work experience in the area.

INJUNCTION - A court order telling a person to do, or not to do, something.

LIEN - The placement of a claim on property or assets when work was completed, but not paid for, by the property or asset owner. The lien gives the business the right to collect money from the sale of the property if sold on a future date.

PERJURY - An untrue comment by a person under oath during a court case.

PLEA - The answer (reply) to the court made by a defendant in a legal disagreement. In most cases a plea includes the defendant asking for less of a punishment or fine.

PRO SE - A person who is part of a court case as a plaintiff or defendant without an attorney. A court case may have a pro se defendant or a pro se plaintiff.

Judgment or Judgment By Default?

A **judgment** is the final decision made by a judge in a legal case after the information and evidence from the plaintiff and the defendant has been presented in a legal case.

A **judgment By default** happens when a plaintiff files a complaint with the court and the defendant is served (given) notice of the legal complaint. The defendant is then legally required to answer (reply) to the court document. The reply may be spoken in person at a court date or a reply may also be written to the court. If the defendant does not reply (in person or in writing) the judge at the court may enter a judgment in the case.
This is known as a default judgment. If the defendant does not respond to the complaint the judge will likely enter a ruling in favor of the plaintiff.

Copyright Protected.   26   www.YMBAgroup.com

The Drawing Board

TOOLBOX

ACQUITTAL   LIEN   JUDGMENT   EVIDENCE   DEFAULT
PLEA   ANSWER   CEASE   CONTEMPT   EXPERT

FIND THESE LEGAL TERMS IN THE WORD SEARCH BELOW

```
T G C P C F S C V A X T T M
J N T E S M O M Y C P L L U
V T E B A N I V K Q N A U O
C W N M T S R A Z U V E A Q
T S M E G L E J H I R N F P
K N M J A D T X Y T D Y E B
W P S K S H U P L T A J D E
T S S M E E W J I A T R W Z
S K D C U O T Z E L J S O W
T T S A W T P T N Q N Q S D
E C N E D I V E O A B I N P
K Y W F W U Y N M V N Z L A
K L F J B J F M V D A E Y V
P D B K E X P E R T A V G K
B L L T R Q A O X D H V D W
S R E W S N A K L E C C P S
```

Shown below are five words from the toolbox whose letters are not correct. Solve the mystery by unscrambling the letters to reveal the correct word.

DECENEVI _____

ELIN _____

RASWEN _____

TERPXE _____

DGUMJNET _____

EXPLORE

Gift or Loan?

A **gift** is when an item is given without any expectation that the person receiving the gift will do something in return. When a gift is given the person who received the gift is not under any requirement to return the gift.

... Consider this ... if person A says to person B, "In three years I think I will buy you a new bicycle." Three years goes by and person B never received a bicycle. Is person A legally required to give the bicycle to person B? ...

The promise to give a gift is not the same as the actual *giving* of a gift. A person who *promises* to give a gift will likely not be legally required to give the gift. But, if the gift was *already given* ... the receiver of the gift can not be required by law to return the gift.

A **loan** is when the person who owns the item agrees to lend it to the other person. The agreement will usually include a specific amount of time to be borrowed and details of how the owner will be compensated (paid).

... Consider this ... Susannah borrows $50 and a video game from Sally. Sally agrees to loan the items to Susannah and requests the money be paid back in 7 days, with the video game being returned the same day as the money. The agreement includes details for the return of the items, so this is a loan, not a gift.

Slander or Libel?

Slander and libel may cause harm to a person's reputation to be harmed as a result of untrue statements. This is a *defamation of character* and hurts a person by changing the public opinion of the person.

Slander - An untrue statement spoken about a person believed to cause harm.

... Consider this ... Jane is late for work and her manager updates the human resources file to show that Jane was late. Jane is upset and makes comments during the day that her manager was late to work today. Jane knows her manager was not late, yet she continues to make the comments to their co-workers. Jane is guilty of slander by saying statements she knows are untrue that harm her manager's reputation.

Libel - An untrue statement written or typed about a person believed to cause harm.

... Consider this ... David and Anthony have a running race. David wins and Anthony is upset that he did not win. Anthony decides to post a sign saying that David cheated in the race. David did not cheat and Anthony is aware of this when he displays the sign Anthony is guilty of libel by writing statements he knows are untrue and harms the opinion the public has of David.

Copyright Protected.   www.YMBAgroup.com

The Drawing Board

Consider the gift and loan details below.
Circle **gift** if it is a gift. Underline **loan** if it is a loan.

1. Jacey is shopping with a friend and asks for $20 to buy a shirt and offers to pay it back in five days. gift   loan

2. Addison borrows $10 and says it will be re-paid next week, but is told it's ok not to pay it back. gift   loan

3. $100 is given in a birthday card. gift   loan

4. A friend offers their bicycle to help get to class for the week while their car is being repaired. gift   loan

5. A book is lost, the neighbor offers their copy and says that there is no rush in it being returned. gift   loan

Consider the libel and slander scenarios below.
Circle slander if it is slander. Circle libel if it is libel.

6. A competitor says Bigo Burgers does not clean its kitchen, but has no facts as details. slander   libel

7. A manager at the sporting goods store tells customers that Huge-Mart does not give refunds to customers (but knows the company offers refunds). slander   libel

8. A letter is mailed to all Zippy car owners by Putt-Putt Motors that says Zippy cars are the most expensive to repair (an untrue statement). slander   libel

9. A college baseball recruiter incorrectly tells a high school senior that the competitor school requires players to pay for their uniforms. slander   libel

THINK

Patent or Copyright?

A **patent** right is given to the inventor of an original idea or design by the United States Patent and Trademark Office (USPTO). Three patent types:

(1) Utility Patent - Protects new product updates or original inventions.
(2) Design Patent - Protects new designs or methods of production.
(3) Plant Patent - Protects the inventors of new and unique plants.

A patent generally protects the inventor for approximately 20 years to give the inventor rights without concern that others will copy, create, or sell the item.

After a patent is issued to the inventor the rights to the item belong to the inventor. However, if someone violates the patent the inventor must begin a legal process to stop the violation. The USPTO does not help the inventor protect their legal rights. The office only gives the inventor the rights for the item. The court system can assist the patent owner in claiming their rights as the patent owner.

A **copyright** is the same idea as a patent, but a copyright is for an idea or creative concept. A copyright is registered by the Copyright Office at the Library of Congress and protects creative works such as books, music, movies and paintings. Creative works are protected, as well as inventions, to encourage people to create and invent. The ability to have the exclusive use of an idea for a period of time motivates people to innovate and design. Innovations and designs help an economy grow and develop to expand and meet the needs and wants of citizens.

Misdemeanor or Felony?

A **misdemeanor** is considered less illegal than a felony.
A misdemeanor is a small violation of the law. The most common result of being found guilty of a misdemeanor is a small to medium amount of money to be paid to the state where the illegal action happened.

... Consider this ... Taylor is from New Jersey and visiting a friend in California. She was walking to the store and crossed the street in the middle of the block rather than walking to the corner and using the crosswalk. A California police officer noticed Taylor and gave a ticket for crossing the street outside of the crosswalk. The ticket was for a misdemeanor and required Taylor to pay a $500 fine for the infraction or to attend a court date in California. An infraction is a violation of a generally minor law.

A **felony** is a medium to large violation of the law. People found guilty of a felony often are sentenced by a judge in court to high fines and to serve time in prison.

... Consider this ... Mathew is backing his car out of a parking space. While exiting the parking space he runs into the sign for the store. The sign is damaged and will need to be entirely replaced. Matthew exits his car, notices what happened, and leaves the parking lot. Matthew is guilty of a felony due to leaving the scene where a $12,500 sign was ruined. The police will use video cameras to research the car that damaged the sign and will then locate Matthew and charge him with a felony.

Copyright Protected.   30   www.YMBAgroup.com

The Drawing Board

Imagine you work in the office of a patent attorney. A patent attorney helps people and businesses get patents for their inventions. A patent attorney will also represent their clients in a courtroom if someone uses the clients patent idea without permission. Using a patent without their permission of the inventor is illegal and known as violating a patent.

UP = Utility Patent   DP = Design Patent   PP = Plant Patent   CR = Copyright

Today you are working to organize customer files for the office. The office uses a specific file system. The first two letters are the type of patent. The next three letters are the company or person last name. The last four are integers to show the year. For example, DP-SMI-2020, would be a design patent for Mr. Smith in 2020. Write the file numbers for the customers below.

1. Goal and Score Company invented an automatic football return system in 2020.
    File Number: __UP__ – __GOA__ – __2020__

2. Bustin' Burgers began to use a new drive-thru burger process in 2018.
    File Number: _____ – _____ – _____

3. Celo Fabrics, Inc. developed a new dark blue dye color in their lab in 2019.
    File Number: _____ – _____ – _____

4. Bunny Hoppers Co. built a machine to fluff fabric in a new way in 2019.
    File Number: _____ – _____ – _____

5. Avenue F Corp. filed for a new type of tree created in their lab in 2018.
    File Number: _____ – _____ – _____

6. The Stars family developed a new type of rose hybrid in their garden in 2020.
    File Number: _____ – _____ – _____

7. Banner Publishing in 2017 created a new United States adventure book.
    File Number: _____ – _____ – _____

8. The poet known as Bhay-Be Rhymz published a poetry collection in 2018.
    File Number: _____ – _____ – _____

9. The Deco brothers created a new shed-in-a-box kit in 2018.
    File Number: _____ – _____ – _____

10. Stellar Construction Inc. improves the dump truck cleaner tool in 2020.
    File Number: _____ – _____ – _____

11. The artist Chere Tamigo presented a new sculpture in 2018.
    File Number: _____ – _____ – _____

12. Baby Beat Music Co. released a birthday music CD in 2020.
    File Number: _____ – _____ – _____

APPLY

Copyright Protected.   www.YMBAgroup.com

Contracts

A contract can help people make agreements and promises in everyday life and in business. The contract will show what is being agreed to and what is expected from those involved in the contract. Common elements to a contract include names, dates, and agreed upon timeframes or dollar amounts.

Legal Contract Terms - An agreement may be made for just about any purpose. However, the terms (details) must be legal and follow the law. For example, Taylor and Jamie can agree that after the lawn is mowed the payment will be $20. They may also legally arrange that rather than a $20 payment Jamie will give Taylor two comic books. The contract terms can not be illegal, so Taylor could not charge Jamie 60% interest on the balance due. Charging very high interest rates is known as *usury* and is illegal.

The two sides that agree in a contract have to each be over 18 years of age. The parties also have to enter the contract without any force, known as entering a contract of their *free-will*.

A Valid Contract Has 5 Features:
(1) Agreement on an Offer
(2) Accepted Terms
(3) Exchange of Items or Actions
(4) Capable Parties
(5) Legal Contract Terms

Brett and Drew want to make a contract for their agreement.
Brett and Drew agree on contract details and create an agreement on an offer.

Agreement on an Offer - Each contract will have two sides, and each side is known as a party to a contract. The sides both need to want to enter into an agreement.

Brett and Drew have talked about what they each will do in the agreement.
Brett and Drew have agreed on the acceptable terms and an exchange of items.

Accepted Terms - After the parties agree to enter into a contract, they are to agree upon the details of the contract. The details of a contract are known as *terms*.

Exchange of Items or Actions - A contract agreement will include the details that if person A does something, person B will do something in return. For example, if the first party in a contract, Taylor, mows the lawn, the second party in the contract, Jamie, will pay Taylor twenty dollars within 14 days or give two comic books.

... Did you know usury is when one party charges an unreasonable amount of interest charges to the person who borrowed money on the balance due.

The Drawing Board

Imagine you are the owner of a car dealership. You recently collected estimates from four car wash businesses in the area. Sparkle Wash was selected as the company to clean the cars on the car lot for your business at the price of $7 per car. You would like a minimum of 10 cars washed per day, but no more than 80 cars washed per week. Car washing will need to be completed during slow times at the business, specifically Monday to Friday between 6 am and 11 am. Washing cars is also permitted Monday to Friday evenings between 8 pm and 10 pm. The contract is one year, January to December. Create the contract you will give to the Sparkle Wash owner to sign as your business agreement. Be creative with your contract terms, but be sure to include the price per car, washing times, and the number or cars to wash each week.

This contract is an agreement between _____ and

_____. The contract will begin on _____

and will end on _____. The company _____

agrees to perform the following services for the car dealership:

Cars will be washed at a rate of _____ each.

Additional contract details are:

Both sides to this contract agree that this is the full agreement between the two sides. Both sides also agree they entered into this agreement on their own without any force, threat, or promises outside this contract.

Date: _____   Date: _____

Signed _____   Signed _____

CREATE

Copyright Protected.   33   www.YMBAgroup.com

Who Can Sign A Contract?

A four-year-old child can write their name on a contract, but is the contract signed by a four year old legal and valid?

Can a four-year-old make a legal promise in a contract? The first requirement to a contract being legal and valid is for the two parties that sign the contract to each be at least 18 years old. The government of the United States set a basic standard for an age when people could be considered mature and aware of their actions to be held responsible for their decisions. Since the legal age to vote in an election in the United States is 18 years old; the age to sign a contract was set to the same age. If someone is younger than 18 years old and wants to enter into a contract, their parent or guardian would need to sign the paperwork for the contract to be legal and valid.

... Did you ever see an advertisement that says, "You must be 18 or older to place an order or call." Purchasing an item is a simple contract. The seller agrees to send you the item shown on the commercial after payment is received. Since purchasing an item is a contract only people 18 and over can enter into the contract agreement created with the purchase legally.

A Contract That is Valid Is A Contract That Is Legal.

Are all adults who are 18 or older able to make a legal promise in a contract?
An adult 18 and older may enter a legal contract if they are generally known to think clearly and reasonably. If someone does not understand the idea of a contract the document signed by this person may not be valid.

Are all contracts signed by clear thinking, reasonable people enforceable?
... Consider this ... Joey had a bicycle accident and went to the hospital. While there Joey was uncomfortable from the injury. A friend gave Joey a contract to sign saying that the friend would be the new owner of Joey's bicycle.

Joey and his friend are both over 18 years of age. Is the contract enforceable? No, in this case Joey was under the care of a doctor and did not sign with a clear mind. The contract would not be enforceable by the friend in a court of law. Joey can choose to keep the bike.

Bilateral — A contract that agrees both person A and person B are both expected to do something.

Unilateral — A contract that agrees person A is expected to do something & receives the contract benefit when complete.

Copyright Protected.

The Drawing Board

Imagine you are a contract attorney. Listed below are some of your clients currently involved in a contract disagreement court case. Review the facts of who signed the contract and circle if the contract is illegal, or if it is most likely legal, and should be enforced.

1. At their tenth birthday party the twins both signed a contract to sell their toys.

    Illegal, so not enforceable   Legal and enforceable

2. During the college graduation 12 graduates signed to attend a class next year.

    Illegal, so not enforceable   Legal and enforceable

3. A contract between members of a retirement community to accept a new fee.

    Illegal, so not enforceable   Legal and enforceable

4. A minor student signs to invite all classmates to a pool party next month.

    Illegal, so not enforceable   Legal and enforceable

5. A 17-year-old signs a contract to buy a friends car when they are 18.

    Illegal, so not enforceable   Legal and enforceable

6. A 19-year-old signs a contest form entry and wins $100.

    Illegal, so not enforceable   Legal and enforceable

7. During a tooth extraction a patient signs to give the dentist a $200 bonus.

    Illegal, so not enforceable   Legal and enforceable

8. A 30-year-old signs a contract to buy all 12-year-olds in town a new book.

    Illegal, so not enforceable   Legal and enforceable

9. While waiting in the emergency room a parent signs to pay the expenses.

    Illegal, so not enforceable   Legal and enforceable

10. A traveler is excited to arrive at the hotel and agrees to pay $1,000 a night.

    Illegal, so not enforceable   Legal and enforceable

11. Do you feel people less than 18 years old should be legally able to sign a contract? Why or why not? What guidelines would you set up for people less than 18 years old to be able to sign a contract? (if any)

STRATEGIZE

Copyright Protected.   35   www.YMBAgroup.com

Contract Enforcement

A contract between two sides is a promise to work together toward a goal. The two sides are expected to follow the details of the contract. If the contract is not followed the law can be used to help enforce the contract agreement. But, did you know there are times when a person who signed a contract may not be legally required to follow the contract agreement? An unenforceable (not valid) contract happens when a contract is signed that includes dishonest ideas, or when one side is forced to sign the agreement.

Misrepresentation is saying, or writing, an idea to give wrong, not correct, information. The person who created the contract either (a) believed what they wrote was true or (b) knew the document was not correct but wrote it anyway. When this happens the person who signed is not required to perform the contract as written.

... Consider this ... Portside Apartments asks for a quote from Squeaky Windows to clean the windows at the apartment community. Portside lists 84 windows. Squeaky offers a bid for 84 windows. Portside creates the contract to read, "Squeaky will clean all the windows at Portside Apartments in one week for $2,000." When Squeaky arrives at the apartment community they realize there are 146 windows. Is the contract enforceable?

The contract is not enforceable. Portside Apartments misrepresented the size of the community on purpose to have a lower price quote. The contract was written to incorrectly list the community as having 84 windows rather than the actual 146 windows.

Duress - A person or business should sign a contract "freely". Freely is when no one is forcing or threatening someone to sign a contract. When a contract is signed under force or threat it is said to be signed under duress.

... Consider this ... USA Music is having a one-day grand opening sale. The primary marketing for the event will be a one-day radio blitz on WPJN. USA Music arrives at WPJN. Ten minutes before the radio blitz for the one day sale is about to begin the radio station manager changes the terms of the deal. The manager says the only way WPJN will do the radio blitz for USA Music is if they sign a contract agreeing to $2,000 worth of advertising on their radio station over the next six months. Is the contract enforceable?

The contract is not enforceable. The USA Music company planned a full marketing campaign around the one day radio blitz at WPJN. The idea of not being able to promote the grand opening minutes before it began was threatening to their business. The contract is not enforceable since signed under duress.

Copyright Protected. 36 www.YMBAgroup.com

The Drawing Board

When two people or businesses decide on an agreement having accurate details is essential. Each side will make a decision to be part of the agreement based on the facts. At times a fact may not be correct by mistake. Other times a fact may be incorrect on purpose to try to encourage the other party to agree to the contract.

Match the facts shown in column A with the misrepresented (untrue) versions of the same facts in column B.

Column A
Misrepresented Fact

Column B
Actual Fact

1. The defendant was never there.

A. No refunds on sale priced items.

2. Buy a car, get free oil changes.

B. Most who enter will win a prize.

3. The car had an oil change last year.

C. The ring is mostly gold.

4. Full refunds given on all purchases.

D. The carpet may be cleaned.

5. Biggest sale of the year.

E. The defendant was not there that day.

6. The ring is 100% real gold.

F. The car had an oil change recently.

7. Carpets are cleaned before move-in.

G. Attend class and try to earn an A.

8. All members get a free ice cream.

H. Largest sale discount of the month.

9. All who enter will win a great prize.

I. Free oil changes for cars over $20,000.

10. Attend class and get an A grade.

J. In 2 years members get an ice cream.

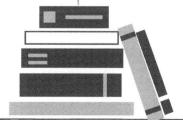

INVESTIGATE

Copyright Protected.   37   www.YMBAgroup.com

Contract Fraud

Fraud

When a person is tricked into signing an agreement based on certain facts, but the contract is an agreement for something else.

... Consider this ... Tracy enjoys making doll beds. A local shop in town is interested in selling the doll beds and provides Tracy with a contract. The shop owner says Tracy will receive 50% of the current price for each bed that sells. Tracy will sell the beds for $40 each and agrees to sign the contract. Tracy receives the first check for $10 from the shop owner showing one bed sold.

...What happened? ... In this scenario the shop owner tricked Tracy into believing the profit would be 50% of the current retail price, $40. The shop owner decided to sell the beds in the store for $20. The contract did not list a sales price, so the store owner picked the price. However, the shop owner committed fraud when Tracy was told the price would be the current $40 price (but then on purpose have a price in the contract).

... Consider this ... Imagine you are a customer at Appliance Kingdom. You are visiting the store today to look for a microwave. You notice a microwave at a low price and ask the owner for more details. The owner of the store explains that he used the microwave a couple times, but decided that a microwave was no longer needed. The microwave is like new, but since it was used, the store is offering a wonderful deal with 50% off, but with no returns accepted. Excited at the great deal you purchase the microwave and take it home. Four days later you want to warm up soup, but the microwave does not turn on. That afternoon you return to the store and tell the sales clerk your experience. The clerk says, "I was wondering who bought that old microwave. We used it in our employee lunch area for two years and it only sometimes worked."

... What happened? ... Although the store has a no returns accepted policy, the law of the state and country is more powerful than the store policy. Since the store owner sold the microwave as like new, hardly used, the true product being purchased was not accurately represented to the customer. Misrepresentation of a product or the terms of a contract can make a purchase contract not enforceable since it is a type of fraud.

Fraud may be either in writing or when speaking untrue facts. Fraud may also be due to leaving out key details on purpose. For example, the owner at Appliance Kingdom could have told the customer, "We have used the microwave for two years in the employee kitchen here at the store." Although this is more accurate of a description the detail of it *only sometimes* working is not included. This is a *material fact.*

> A contract may be unenforceable when a material (important) fact is intentionally (on purpose) not told to the other party (side) of a contract.

Copyright Protected.   38   www.YMBAgroup.com

The Drawing Board

"Swim in clean water with the Tropical Pool Cleaner."
"Only $175.95 for clean pool water all summer!"

Last year Tropical Pool Club advertised in the local paper a new pool cleaner. The pool cleaner was advertised as removing 90% of pool debris in less than six hours. Five different customers purchased the pool cleaner and removed their current pool cleaner system to install the Tropical Pool Club Cleaner. Over the next three months each of the five customers were not happy with the product. First, they each reported the pool cleaner required four days to bring the water to a clean level. This was much more than the advertised six hours. When the store owner was asked he replied, "Yes, its true, most pools will take four days." The customers believed this to be a fraud. Then, after 90 days, the homeowners each noticed oil in the pool. The motor for the cleaner had a defect (problem) that caused it to put oil into the pool. The result is unclean pool water and oil on the pool walls. The store owner suggested the homeowners have Spiffy Clean Company visit to clean each pool. Spiffy Clean charges .45 cents per gallon to clean oil off the sides of the pool, re-fill with new water and balance the pool chemical levels.

The Plaintiff is the five homeowners. They are requesting:
(1) Tropical Pool Club refund the cost of the pool cleaner.
(2) Tropical Pool Club pays for the cost to clean each of the pools with Spiffy Clean.
(3) Tropical Pool Club installs a new pool cleaner for free to the five pools.

Complete the chart below to show the total dollar amount asked for in this case.

Customer	Gallons		Cost Per Gallon		Pool Cleaner		Total
1	(9,000	×	.45)	+	175.95	=	$ _____
2	(10,000	×	.45)	+	175.95	=	$ _____
3	(7,000	×	.45)	+	175.95	=	$ _____
4	(12,000	×	.45)	+	175.95	=	$ _____
5	(15,000	×	.45)	+	175.95	=	$ _____

6. Total Damages (money) Requested By Plaintiff: $ _____
7. Imagine you are the judge. What is your verdict?

COMPUTE

Copyright Protected.   39   www.YMBAgroup.com

Individual Torts

TORT A
Shawn is upset that someone else won the running race. Shawn surprises the winner by grasping the winner's wrist to ask them to race again.

TORT B
Bobbie arrives at the state fair and notices two people wearing the same outfit. Bobbie says the other outfits are stolen knowing it is untrue.

What is a tort?

Tort in the French language is the same as the English word *wrong*. A tort is the legal term used when something unwanted is done to a person or a persons property. A tort is often the reason for a civil (not for a criminal) lawsuit. When a person experiences humiliation (embarrassment), or is harmed by another person's actions, a tort has been done against a person.

TORT C
Max just found out about a party but did not receive an invitation. Max writes statements on the internet he knows are not true about the person hosting the party.

TORT E
Eddie borrowed a library book. Inside were photos of a person that lives in town. The person is wearing an embarrassing costume and looks silly. Eddie sends the picture in an email to over 50 friends on the computer.

TORT D
Daryl was upset with a stranger at the movies. Daryl says mean words and makes rude expressions to hurt the stranger's feelings.

A tort done to a person includes the following illegal actions:

(a) **A**ssault or Battery - threats to touch, or actual touching, to cause harm.

(b) **S**lander - saying something untrue that causes a person harm.

(c) **L**ibel - writing something untrue that causes a person harm.

(d) **I**ntent to hurt - cause emotional pain, extremely hurtful actions that causes harm.

(e) **P**rivacy violations - including sharing private information causing humiliation or harm

One purpose of the law is to protect and assist people who are harmed. When a tort is done against a person the courts and the legal system are available to help the injured person.
A lawsuit provides the harmed person an opportunity to receive money or to have their items returned.

Defamation
Saying (slander) or writing (libel) untrue statements that hurt a person.

Copyright Protected.   www.YMBAgroup.com

The Drawing Board

The legal system is available to assist people or businesses that have been unfairly treated or hurt under the law. However, not all actions that result in unfair treatment or hurt are illegal torts. When a person or business makes an unpopular decision or does not demonstrate manners, a law is not always broken. A person or business hurt by these actions could have a difficult case to prove in a court of law. Although not kind, a person or business being rude or hurtful may not be violating (breaking) the law.

Let's play Tort-Tic-Tac-Toe! Review each scenario. Write **TORT** if the action is an **illegal** wrong that caused harm to a person or business. Write **UNETHICAL** if it was **not illegal**, but it was not a fair or kind way to treat a person or business.

Crystal Conditioner Inc. writes an advertisement without any facts saying that the competitor has glass in the hair products. _____	A jogger in the rain is waiting to cross a busy street. Cars drive by and do not stop. _____	When JC is running to catch a bus two people get pushed down and need to stay in the hospital for one night. _____
At the zoo a person on line tells people to let them cut the line ... or else. _____	A competitor company to Gr8 Shakes, Inc. tells customers they think Gr8 Shakes are not yummy. _____	At the office party two managers say they are better workers than all co-workers at the party. _____
A new song is reviewed on the radio and the announcer says the song is a copy to an older song from 1974.	Two children are talking at the park. One child says the scooter for the other child is dented, old and looks boring to ride.	People at the park are talking. A person walking by is hurt by comments overheard.

Examine your results.
Can you draw a line to make a Tort-Tick-Tac-Toe?

EXPLORE

Property Torts

When an action by one person causes another person to feel hurt, or to lose an item of value, a tort has likely been done. However, a tort may also be done to something that is owned by a person or business. In legal terms property refers to anything that you can own. Included is land or a home, but also included in the property category is anything you can touch. Eyeglasses to computers, books to a car are all items that may be the subject of a tort complaint. Personal property may only be used with the permission of the owner.

A Property Tort Includes:

(A) Borrowing an item and not returning the item.

(B) Breaking an item includes the careless use of an item.

(C) Using an item without permission.

(D) Entering a location without permission.

A student borrowed a basketball from the coach for one night. The student decided to keep the ball.

The neighbors were on vacation. The garden hose was left in the yard. Each morning for five days the hose was used to water the lawn next door until the neighbors returned.

A friend borrowed a car to go to the store. At the store the friend left the keys in the car and went inside. The car was not there when the friend came out of the store.

The water park closed for the winter season. A former employee jumped over the fence to take pictures of the empty park.

If a tort is being committed against someone's property the owner of the property must follow the law when seeking a solution. Consider this example: A homeowner notices the fruit from the garden is being picked by children who jump over the fence each day. Should the homeowner place snakes in the garden or leave an aggressive dog in the yard? Certainly not. The homeowner may not cause a tort against the fence jumpers even though they are committing a tort by entering the property and taking the fruit of the landowner. The legal system is available to assist the owner.

Copyright Protected.   42   www.YMBAgroup.com

The Drawing Board

Review each tort scenario below. Label each as either A, B, C or D to indicate the type of tort is being described.

A	B	C	D
Did not return a borrowed item.	Broke or damaged a borrowed item.	Used an item without the owner's permission.	Entered a location without permission.

A, B, C, and D are torts that may be done to property.

1. While working on a movie set an actor decides to try a camera. During the lunch break the actor takes pictures using the camera.
    The property tort best described here is letter: _____
2. A student checks out books from a library and decides to keep the books beyond the return by date.
    The property tort best described here is letter: _____
3. The boat rental company is closed on Tuesday. A visitor decides to drive a boat on the lake while walking by on a Tuesday.
    The property tort best described here is letter: _____ and _____
4. Two friends agree to trade sports equipment for one week. When they meet to return the items friend 1 tells friend 2 the tennis racquet broke so they did not plan to return it since it was not able to be used any longer.
    The property tort best described here are letters: _____ and _____
5. On a walk a family decides to use a neighbors swing set while the neighbors are on vacation.
    The property tort best described here is letter: _____
6. The pizza delivery person bought pizza to RPE Motor Sales and noticed new car keys on the counter. The delivery person decided to take the keys and take the new car for a drive around the parking lot.
    The property tort best described here is letter: _____
7. A family rented an RV from Fun RV Company. The RV is to be returned May 18. The family decides to keep the RV until July 4 and does not tell the company.
    The property tort best described here is letter: _____ and _____
8. While on vacation a hotel guest rents a bicycle for the day. When the bike rental clerk is checking in the returned bicycle they notice the basket is broken.
    The property tort best described here is letter: _____

THINK

Copyright Protected.   www.YMBAgroup.com

Court Case Procedures

In the United States a court case in any city, state, or federal court will generally follow the same pattern of events. The steps of each case are shown below. A standard order of events will help keep the focus of the case on the evidence and the violations of the law. The courtroom operates in an organized and reliable style. The steps of each court jury case are generally the same for each defendant.

The defendant is served (given) papers to show the details of the legal complaint of the plaintiff.

↓

The lawyer for the defendant and the lawyer for the plaintiff review the evidence.

↓

If there will be a jury, the "voir dire" process is completed and jurors are selected.

↓

The courtroom trial begins.

↓

The lawyer for the plaintiff makes an opening statement to the courtroom and jury.

↓

The lawyer for the defendant makes an opening statement to the courtroom and jury.

↓

The lawyers for both sides question plaintiff witnesses in front of the jury.

↓

The lawyers for both sides question defendant witnesses in front of the jury.

↓

The lawyer for the plaintiff makes a closing statement to the courtroom and jury.

↓

The lawyer for the defendant makes a closing statement to the courtroom and jury.

↓

The judge orders the jury to consider the facts presented in the trial and to make a decision.

↓

The jury foreperson will provide the judge with their decision after it is reached.

↓

The jury foreperson will read the decision aloud in court for the plaintiff and defendant to hear.

↓

The judge will make a ruling on jail time and the monetary fines, if any.

↓

The defendant will be free (if found innocent) or will need to follow the judges ruling (if found guilty)

Copyright Protected.

The Drawing Board

Imagine you are the attorney for the plaintiff. Listed below are eleven steps that commonly happen when there is a legal dispute in the court. Place a number between 1 to 11 to organize the items into the correct order of events. The final result will be the judges ruling.

1. _____ If there will be a jury, the voir dire process is completed, and jurors are selected.

2. _____ The lawyer for the plaintiff makes a closing statement to the courtroom and jury.

3. _____ The defendant is served papers with the details of why the plaintiff began a lawsuit.

4. _____ The lawyer for the plaintiff makes an opening statement to the courtroom and jury.

5. _____ The jury foreperson will provide the judge with their decision after it is reached.

6. _____ The courtroom trial begins.

7. _____ The jury foreperson reads the decision in court for the plaintiff and defendant to hear.

8. _____ Plaintiff witnesses are questioned by the lawyers for both sides in front of the jury.

9. _____ The judge orders the jury to consider the facts from the trial and to make a decision.

10. _____ The judge decides a ruling on the jail time or fines for the defendant if guilty.

11. _____ If guilty, the defendant will need to follow the judge's decision.

INVESTIGATE

Copyright Protected.　　　45　　　www.YMBAgroup.com

Opening and Closing Statements

The Opening Statement

The Opening Statement is the introduction to the court case. The attorney for the defendant, and the attorney for the plaintiff, will tell the court what they will explain during the trial. Each side will present a quick idea of the topics they will cover, the evidence they will show, and the result they would like when the trial is over. The opening statement by the defendant attorney will often include a summary of the law. The summary of the law that applies to the trial will explain to the jury that the defendant must be found innocent if the plaintiff evidence is not able to prove guilt.

The Closing Statement

The Closing Statement is presented at the end of a court trial. After the plaintiff and the defendant have shown their evidence to the court, and called the witnesses to the stand, a summary of the trial begins. The plaintiff attorney gives a summary of the courtroom events during the trial and why they feel it supports the case. Next, the defense attorney will present a closing statement. The statement will include what the state did not prove with the evidence. The defendant attorney will also explain the reasons why they feel their client should be found not guilty.

After the closing statements the judge will remind the jury of the law that applies to the court case. The jury will go to a room together and discuss the court case. This is called *jury deliberation*. When the jury agrees on the guilt or innocence of the defendant the judge will receive the decision in writing.

Rules of Evidence

The *rules of evidence* are guidelines to tell the plaintiff and defendant attorney's what is allowed and what is not allowed, to be presented in a trial as evidence. There are specific steps that have to be followed when gathering and holding evidence. There are also particular rules about what items are able to be considered evidence. The rules are in place to make sure the items used to find a person guilty or innocent are accurate and reliable. Evidence is often used to find a person guilty of a crime. Since evidence is so important it needs to be reliable so an innocent person will not be judged as guilty. For this reason, a plan for how evidence should be managed has been created to detail which evidence may be used in court.

The Drawing Board

A person has received a written complaint saying they are accused of taking two video games from a store without paying for the items. Review the case facts and complete the opening statements for the court date.

Plaintiff and Defendant Agree On The Following Facts In The Case:

- ☐ The defendant is accused of taking two video games from the store without paying.
- ☐ The date and location of the alleged event was November 30 in Chicago, Illinois.
- ☐ That day the defendant left work at 5:15 pm and arrived at the video game store at 5:35 pm.
- ☐ The store security found the two video games in the defendants shopping bag at 5:50 pm.
- ☐ The two video games did not have any fingerprints of the defendant.
- ☐ The defendant did purchase two video games and earned a coupon for one free video game.
- ☐ The defendant visits the store an average of twice per week during the past eight months.
- ☐ The brother of the defendant was working as the cashier at the store on November 30.

Imagine you are the attorney for the defendant. Write your opening statement.

Be sure to include why the facts of the case *do not* prove your client as guilty.

Let the jury know what you would like their decision to be in the case.

I Defend The Accused

Imagine you are the attorney for the plaintiff. Write your opening statement.

Be sure to include how the facts of the case *do* prove the defendant is guilty.

Let the jury know what you would like their decision to be in the case.

I Represent The Store

APPLY

Copyright Protected.   47   www.YMBAgroup.com

The Jury

The United States Constitution states that an accused person in some circumstances will have the right to a jury trial. The jury will be made up of people that are local citizens who will decide the guilt or innocence of the defendant. But what does that mean?

A jury is a group of randomly selected people being brought together to work as a team during a court trial. The state or federal government may use a list of registered voters or state-issued identification cards to select the people chosen to be considered for a jury. People being considered as jurors on the case will be asked to visit the courthouse on a specific day and time. Once at the courthouse the potential juror will meet with the lawyer for both the plaintiff and the defendant. This process is known as *voir dire*.

The lawyers will ask each possible juror questions about their ideas, background, experiences, and beliefs. The two lawyers will work together to agree on which people will serve as jurors on the pending legal case. A completed jury most commonly has between 6 and 12 people. The jury will be expected to listen and look at the evidence carefully. The jury will then use what they see and hear to compare it to the guidelines and rules in the law. The jury will decide the guilt or innocence of the defendant.

Jury Terms

Voir dire - The process of questioning potential jurors as the attorneys for each side of a lawsuit seeking to approve a set of jurors for the trial.

Foreperson - The jury will agree on a leader to speak on behalf of the jury to the court. The goal of one point of contact between the jury and the courtroom is to help the communication be more efficient. The foreperson helps organize jurors to agree on an idea, decision, or question, before presenting a final result to the court.

Jury Duty - A possible juror will receive a summons in the mail requiring the person to be at the courthouse on a specific date and time to be considered as a juror.

Jury Summons - A legal document sent to a person that requires the person to attend the courthouse at a specific date and time. If unable to be there the person being considered as a jury must reply with an explanation of why they can not attend.

Copyright Protected. 48 www.YMBAgroup.com

The Drawing Board

Case Details and Facts

TOOLBOX

A 28 year old borrowed five pieces of scuba equipment from a store. The items included (a) a wetsuit (b) an air tank (c) an underwater camera (d) a bag and (e) an underwater watch. The items were to be returned to the store in four days. The defendant claims that while at the beach the underwater camera did not work and the wetsuit was ripped. The plaintiff (the store) believes that items were all in working condition when they left the store with the defendant. The store seeks to collect the cost to replace the camera and the wet suit, $450, from the defendant.

Imagine you are the attorney for the defendant. Listed below are seven people being considered to join the jury for the case. As the defendant's attorney place a check (✓) in the accept box if you find the person acceptable as a possible juror. If the person is not acceptable as a juror place an X in the decline box.

1. Juror 1, Male, 38, owns a fishing boat and has a charter business.

    Accept As A Juror ☐   Decline As A Juror ☐

2. Juror 2, Female, 57, said all businesses take advantage of customers.

    Accept As A Juror ☐   Decline As A Juror ☐

3. Juror 3, Male, 42, attended the same college as the scuba store owner.

    Accept As A Juror ☐   Decline As A Juror ☐

4. Juror 4, Female, 35, calls all extreme sports fans, *Wacky*.

    Accept As A Juror ☐   Decline As A Juror ☐

5. Juror 5, Female, 23, rented equipment from the store and all was fine.

    Accept As A Juror ☐   Decline As A Juror ☐

6. Juror 6, Female, 68, a retired small business owner.

    Accept As A Juror ☐   Decline As A Juror ☐

7. Juror 7, Male, 51, works as a bank manager and enjoys movies.

    Accept As A Juror ☐   Decline As A Juror ☐

STRATEGIZE

Copyright Protected.   www.YMBAgroup.com

Supreme Court Cases

The Supreme Court of the United States is the top court of the country. A lawyer often presents decisions on court cases made by the Supreme Court as a reason why the court should judge the court case in their favor. Typically a court case has one judge to decide on a case. But The Supreme Court has nine judges who listen to the facts in a case and vote on the final decision. The side of the case with the higher number of judicial (judges) votes is considered the winner of the court case.

Precedent - A decision by a court that becomes a reason for innocence in a future legal case.

Gibbons v. Ogden
Year: 1824

Summary: In 1824 there was a disagreement between a business owner in New Jersey, Mr. Gibbons, and a business owner in New York, Mr. Ogden. The owner from New Jersey wanted to have water access in New York to transport items for his company.

Plaintiff: Mr. Gibbons was a business owner in New Jersey who was given a permit by the United States Federal Government to use the United States waters to transport his goods.

Defendant: Mr. Ogden was an investor in the New York Steamship Company. The New York Steamship Company granted Mr. Ogden permission to use the New York waters to transport his goods.

Dispute: New York stated that only Mr. Ogden could use the New York waters to transport his goods for sale. The federal government said Mr. Gibbons could use the waters in the United States. But New York is in the United States.

Question: Who has the right to control access to the waters within a state? Does the state have the right over the water inside its boundaries, or does the federal government?

Supreme Court Decision: The court decided that when a company sells and buys goods across state boundaries that the United States Federal Government has the complete power to oversee and regulate (manage) the activities.

The Drawing Board

The United States Constitution allows for court cases to change the laws that are to be followed by citizens and businesses. When one court case ends similar disputes in the future may apply the judges' decision to understand the law better. Imagine you are the judge, and you call your court to order. Consider the created sample case and write your decision below.

Plaintiff: Southeast Truck and Transport Company

CASE PRECEDENT GIBBONS V. OGDEN

Defendant: State of Alabama

Dispute: A company from the state of Alabama travels across highways in Georgia on the way to a customer in South Carolina. The trucks carry heavy equipment, and Alabama is concerned the constant weight causes damage to the highway. The state has asked the company to no longer travel on the Alabama roads. The company believes the state does not have a right to restrict who may, or who may not, travel on the state roads.

Question: Does a state have the right to decide who can use the state roads?

Which of the 27 amendments to the United States Constitution apply to this case?

Amendment _____ says _____.

You are the judge. Circle your verdict below. What is your decision? What facts of the case led to your decision? What amendments to the Constitution support your decision? What other thoughts or reasons do you have for your decision?

    Judges Verdict: Agrees with the Plaintiff   Agrees with the Defendant

_____
_____
_____
_____
_____

THINK

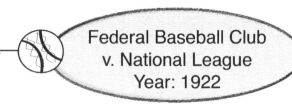

Federal Baseball Club v. National League
Year: 1922

Summary: In 1922 a lawsuit was begun by the Federal League because they felt their league was forced to close down by a competitor baseball group, the National League. A league in baseball is a group of teams that play games against each other. The leagues charge an attendance fee at the stadiums when people come to watch the baseball games.

Plaintiff: Federal Baseball Club

Defendant: National League Baseball

Dispute: National baseball in the United States currently has two leagues, the National and the American. In 1915 there were also teams playing in another league known as the Federal. The professional baseball industry around 1915 was trying to organize to have two leagues, only the National and the American. The owners of the Federal league were unhappy with their league not being included, and as a result, closed down.

Question: By trying to organize to two leagues was the baseball industry creating a monopoly?

Supreme Court Decision: The defendant, National League Baseball, was found guilty of pushing the Federal League out of the professional baseball industry. But, the Supreme Court also decided that baseball is not a business that operates across state lines. The defendants were fined $240,000 as a penalty for the efforts to make a baseball monopoly.

Do you agree with the Supreme Court decision in the Federal Baseball Club case?

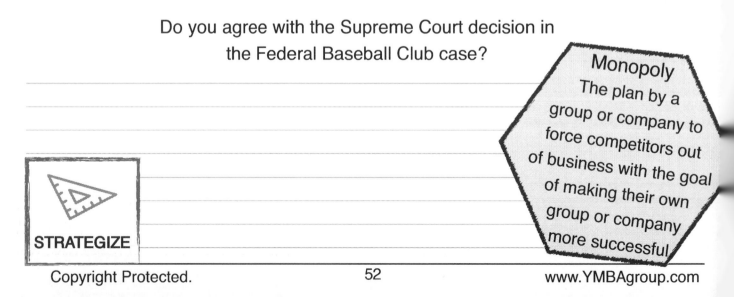

Monopoly
The plan by a group or company to force competitors out of business with the goal of making their own group or company more successful

STRATEGIZE

The Drawing Board

After successfully making a decision on your morning case, you return to the judge's chambers. The afternoon docket (schedule) has begun. Imagine the legal case below is your second item of the day's schedule. Consider the details of the created case and write your decision below.

CASE PRECEDENT: FEDERAL BASEBALL V. NATIONAL LEAGUE

Plaintiff: Pizza Pal Co.

Defendant: American Pizza, Inc. and Pie For You Corporation

Dispute: A small family business, Pizza Pal, believes that the reason their store is not successful is due to large, national pizza brands having so many locations. Pizza Pal believes the many locations of the national brand create a monopoly making it hard for new businesses to be successful. The two national brands named in the complaint disagree. The national brands state they are not in any way, making it difficult for Pizza Pal to have a successful pizza business.

Question: Does a successful business create a monopoly preventing new competitors from entering the marketplace?

Which of the 27 amendments to the United States Constitution apply to this case?

Amendment _____ says _____.

You are the judge. Circle your verdict below. What is your decision? What facts of the case led to your decision? What amendments support your decision? What other thoughts or reasons do you have for your decision?

Judges Verdict: Agrees with the Plaintiff   Agrees with the Defendant

_____
_____
_____
_____
_____

EXPLORE

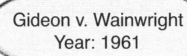

Gideon v. Wainwright
Year: 1961

$ $ $ $ $ $ $ $

Summary: In 1961, a man, Mr. Gideon, was arrested and was going to be on trial. If at the end of the trial, he was found guilty he was going to spend many years in jail. Mr. Gideon could not afford to pay an attorney to help in his defense during the trial.

Plaintiff: Mr. Gideon

Defendant: Mr. Wainwright

Dispute: The plaintiff, Mr. Gideon, was going to be on trial and asked the court system to provide him an attorney. The courts decided not to provide an attorney. Mr. Gideon had to be his own attorney in the court trial and was found guilty. Mr. Gideon appealed the decision to the Supreme Court saying he did not receive a fair trial.

Question: When a person is going to be on trial should there be a requirement for the court to provide an attorney?

Supreme Court Decision: The Supreme Court decided that the sixth amendment to the United States Constitution required the courts to provide an attorney. The court stated that when a person is not able to afford their own attorney and is on trial where a guilty verdict may result in a year of jail or longer, the court must provide an attorney.

Do you agree with this decision made by the Supreme Court?

EXPLORE

Copyright Protected.   www.YMBAgroup.com

The Drawing Board

It is 9 am, and your court schedule is very busy today. Your first case reminds you of the Supreme Court case Gideon v. Wainwright. You are sure to mention the verdict of that case when writing your decision on the case below.

Consider the pretend dispute presented this morning and write your decision on the case.

Plaintiff: Minor under 18 years of age

Defendant: Parents of Plaintiff, a minor.

Dispute: A minor under age 18 is on trial for a crime. The parents of the minor arranged for an attorney for their child. The child does not think the attorney is doing a good job. The minor asks the court to arrange for a lawyer paid for by the state instead of the parents. The state does not believe the cost should be taken from taxpayer money since the parents can pay for the attorney. The parents believe the lawyer they selected is doing a good job.

Question: Can an accused person choose not to pay for their own lawyer if they can afford to pay for the attorney? Can a minor choose their own attorney?

Which of the 27 amendments to the United States Constitution apply to this case?

Amendment _____ says _____.

You are the judge. Circle your verdict below. What is your decision? What facts of the case led to your decision? What amendments to the Constitution support your decision? What other thoughts or reasons do you have for your decision?

    Judges Verdict: Agrees with the Plaintiff   Agrees with the Defendant

_____
_____
_____
_____
_____
_____

APPLY

Tinker v. Des Moines
Year: 1969

Summary: In 1969 two students, Mr. Tinker and Ms. Tinker, decided to wear a band around their arm to share their opinion on the Vietnam War. The school asked the two students to take off the armbands. The students did not want to take off the armbands and were suspended from attending school for not obeying the request of the teacher and principal.

Plaintiffs: Mr. Tinker, Ms. Tinker, were both minors (a minor is someone less than age 18)

Defendant: Des Moines Public School System

Dispute: The two students wanted to wear armbands to show their opinion on the Vietnam War. The school stated that the armbands created a distraction and not all agreed with opinion being made by the armbands.

Question: Freedom of speech is a right of Americans in the Constitution. Do students lose their rights when they enter a schoolhouse? If yes, the students were to remove the armbands when asked. If no, the students should have been able to wear the armbands and the suspension from school was illegal.

Supreme Court Decision: The Supreme Court decision was to allow students to wear the armbands. The decision stated that rights granted by the Constitution are not lost when a student enters a school building. Freedom of speech applies to the person, not the location.

Do you agree with this decision made by the Supreme Court?

The Drawing Board

Today your morning schedule was clear and did not have cases. This afternoon your first case to consider is a complex pretend case. Three people under age 18, and their school district, are asking for assistance in settling a legal dispute.

Plaintiff: A minor, under 18 years of age

Defendant: Mountainside High School, Rock County

CASE PRECEDENT TINKER V. DES MOINES

Dispute: A student at a local high school has a very specific fashion style. The student chooses only to wear t-shirts showing the name of a company that supports freedom in the United States. Beginning in grade 5 the student would wear a t-shirt supporting one of these businesses each day. The school just passed a regulation requiring students not to wear logos or brands on their clothes at school. The plaintiff is suing the school to have the right to choose their own clothes and to keep the freedom to make a statement with what they wear. The public school (supported by tax dollars) believes it is private property so they can direct students in what to wear.

Question: Can a public school district tell a student not to wear logos or brands?

Which of the 27 amendments to the United States Constitution apply to this case?

Amendment _____ says _____.

You are the judge. Circle your verdict below. What is your decision? What facts of the case led to your decision? What amendments to the Constitution support your decision? What other thoughts or reasons do you have for your decision?

    Judges Verdict: Agrees with the Plaintiff   Agrees with the Defendant

_____
_____
_____
_____
_____

APPLY

Copyright Protected.   57   www.YMBAgroup.com

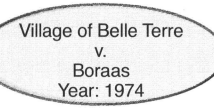

Village of Belle Terre v. Boraas
Year: 1974

Summary: In 1974 a group of students from a local college rented a home in the Village of Belle Terre. The village had a rule about the number of unrelated people who may live in the same home.

Plaintiff: Village of Belle Terre

Defendant: Mr. Boraas

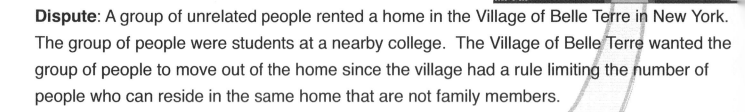

Dispute: A group of unrelated people rented a home in the Village of Belle Terre in New York. The group of people were students at a nearby college. The Village of Belle Terre wanted the group of people to move out of the home since the village had a rule limiting the number of people who can reside in the same home that are not family members.

Question: Is it legal for a residential neighborhood to limit the number of unrelated (not family) people who reside (live) in the same home?

Supreme Court Decision: The Supreme Court decided that a community could limit the number of unrelated people who permanently lived at a home inside the community. The rule was put in place by the community with the goal of creating a quiet neighborhood and did not restrict who could visit members of the community. Limiting large numbers of non-family members living at the same address was approved as a decision allowed by the village.

Do you agree with this decision made by the Supreme Court?

THINK

The Drawing Board

Today is Thursday, and your first case is over a similar question as discussed by the Supreme Court in Boraas v. Belle Terre. The decision of the court in 1974 on this case will certainly offer support for your decision on the current legal dispute. Consider the created scenario below and write your decision on the case.

Plaintiff: The Woof Walkers Inc.

Defendant: Aspen Ridge Shores Homeowners Association

CASE PRECEDENT BORAAS V. BELLE TERRE

Dispute: Aspen Ridge Shores Homeowners Association represents a community of 812 homes. The community is generally quiet and has many walking trails for the members of the community. The plaintiff is a business owned by residents of the community that offers dog walking services. The Woof Walkers recently began watching customers dogs at their home. The home produces a constant barking and disrupts the quiet neighborhood. The dogs visit the community dog park for many hours and prevent homeowners from visiting the dog park due to the high number of dogs regularly brought by the plaintiff. The community has sent a letter telling the Woof Walkers they may not have more than two dogs in their home or at the dog park.

Question: Can a community homeowners association restrict how many dogs may live in a privately owned home? Can the use of the dog park be restricted?

Which of the 27 amendments to the United States Constitution apply to this case?

Amendment _____ says _____.

You are the judge. Circle your verdict below. What is your decision? What facts of the case led to your decision? What amendments to the Constitution support your decision? What other thoughts or reasons do you have for your decision?

    Judges Verdict: Agrees with the Plaintiff   Agrees with the Defendant

_____

_____

_____

APPLY

Texas v. Johnson
Year: 1989

Summary: In 1989 Mr. Johnson attended a political event where he burned an American flag while making a statement. Many people were offended and considered the burning of the flag an act against the government. The state of Texas arrested Mr. Johnson, who was later convicted of burning a symbol of the country.

Plaintiff: State of Texas

Defendant: Mr. Johnson

Dispute: Mr. Johnson believed the burning of the flag while making a statement was his right and freedom granted by the Constitution. The state of Texas disagreed with Mr. Johnson and did not believe freedom of speech did not include objects and symbols.

Question: Is the use of symbols when making a statement considered freedom of speech that is guaranteed to all United States citizens in the first amendment to the Constitution?

Supreme Court Decision: The Supreme Court decided that the use of symbols when making a statement is included in the free speech granted to citizens by the first amendment of the Constitution. The defendant, Mr. Johnson, had the conviction overturned and was not guilty.

What happens when a case is overturned?

___

Do you agree with this decision made by the Supreme Court?

___

Overturned
When a decision made by one court of law is changed and reversed by another court of law.

EXPLORE

The Drawing Board

Today is Friday, the last day of the workweek. Your schedule only has one case on the docket today. The legal matter is based on the protection provided by the first amendment, freedom of speech. Consider the pretend legal case presented to you below and write your decision on the case.

Plaintiff: Pine County High School

Defendant: The debate club at Pine County High School

CASE PRECEDENT TEXAS V. JOHNSON

Dispute: On the last day of school twelve members of the high school debate club gathered outside with their notebooks. The notebooks were purchased by each student using their own money. When the last school bell rang the students began to rip the notebooks into as many little, tiny pieces as possible. A school employee told the students to stop and called the police. The school said the students created a disrespectful scene and caused damage to the property. The school also said that students do not have permission to cause damage to items on school property.

Question: Can a public school tell a student not to damage their own property? Which of the 27 amendments to the United States Constitution apply to this case?

Amendment _____ says _____.

You are the judge. Circle your verdict below. What is your decision? What facts of the case led to your decision? What amendments to the Constitution support your decision? What other thoughts or reasons do you have for your decision?

   Judges Verdict: Agrees with the Plaintiff   Agrees with the Defendant

INVESTIGATE

Copyright Protected. 61 www.YMBAgroup.com

Y.M.B.A. Business Law Review

Congratulations on completing the Y.M.B.A. Business Law workbook. Consider the questions below to demonstrate all you have learned. Write your answers in the spaces provided on page 66.

1. The legal process is set up to help find solutions to:
   (A) Puzzles (B) Disputes (C) Riddles (D) Math

2. Which can not be a party in a court of law?
   (A) People (B) A Town (C) A Family Pet (D) A Business

3. The Congress and House of Representatives _____ the laws.
   (A) Create (B) Approve (C) Judge (D) Veto

4. The United States government has _____ branches of government.
   (A) 3 (B) 9 (C) 10 (D) 27

5. Some laws in the United States were taken from ideas in The _____ Empire.
   (A) Greek (B) Roman (C) Ottoman (D) American

6. A President reviews a bill when considering a new law and can:
   (A) Change Details (B) Approve (C) Veto (D) Ignore

7. The laws from which court is stronger from the laws from the other courts?
   (A) Village (B) County (C) State (D) Federal

8. Which court would oversee a legal dispute between two states?
   (A) Village (B) County (C) State (D) Federal

9. Which is not an Article in the United States Constitution?
   (A) The President (B) The Judges (C) The States (D) The Evidence

10. The first amendment in The Bill of Rights is on the topic of:

   (A) Freedom   (B) Animals   (C) Voting Power (D) Land

11. The 22nd Amendment says a President can only be elected _____ times.

   (A) One   (B) Two   (C) Three   (D) Four

12. A contract is valid when two parties over 18 years old have agreed on:

   (A) Ink Color   (B) Paper Size   (C) Terms   (D) Banks

13. Charging a very high-interest rate on a loan is illegal and is called:

   (A) Slander   (B) Pro Se   (C) Usury   (D) Libel

14. A contract that requires both sides to do something is a _____ contract.

   (A) Illegal   (B) Uni-Lateral   (C) Government (D) Bi-Lateral

15. An important fact in a court case is called a _____ fact.

   (A) Popular   (B) Majority   (C) Material   (D) Fabric

16. An employee tells co-workers untrue facts about their manager. This is:

   (A) Slander   (B) Libel   (C) Investing   (D) Evidence

17. Slander and libel are examples of:

   (A) Defamation   (B) Assault   (C) Permission   (D) Usury

18. Documents, pictures and items related to a case are kept in the _____ room.

   (A) Judges   (B) Evidence   (C) Court   (D) Jury

19. Which court would have more than one judge overseeing a court case?

   (A) Village   (B) Local   (C) State   (D) National

20. Which of the following would be the name of a document in a lawsuit?

   (A) Syllabus   (B) Complaint   (C) Question   (D) Evaluation

Copyright Protected.   63   www.YMBAgroup.com

21. The person asking an appeals court to review a verdict is a:

(A) Bailiff (B) Juror (C) Appellant (D) Stenographer

22. The Supreme Court of the United States has _____ judges decide each case.

(A) 3 (B) 5 (C) 7 (D) 9

23. A court order to immediately stop an action is called a _____ and desist.

(A) Cease (B) Resist (C) Reply (D) Discover

24. A defendant does not appear for a court date or send a reply. The judge issues a:

(A) Summary (B) Notice (C) Warning (D) Default Judgment

25. Which of the following is least likely to give a loan:

(A) Library (B) Bank (C) Friend (D) Restaurant

26. A newspaper prints an article with details presented as facts that are wrong is:

(A) Slander (B) Libel (C) Information (D) Evidence

27. An artist sculpts a new statue from clay and registers with the USPTO office for a:

(A) Design Patent (B) Utility Patent (C) Copyright (D) Trademark

28. The same artist improves the sculpting clay to dry slower and registers for a:

(A) Plant Patent (B) Utility Patent (C) Award (D) Copyright

29. A 16 year old signs a contract to babysit Monday. Why is this not enforceable?

(A) Age of Signor (B) Ink Color (C) Contract Reason (D) Day of the Week

30. An Oregon resident gets a ticket in Idaho and is asked to attend a court date in:

(A) Oregon (B) Ohio (C) Idaho (D) Washington, D.C

Copyright Protected. 64 www.YMBAgroup.com

31. The final decision in a court of law is known as a:

    (A) Opinion (B) Verdict (C) Complaint (D) Veto

32. A private school does not accept a student to the school is:

    (A) Libel (B) An Appeal (C) A Tort (D) Not Illegal

33. A Supreme Court judge most likely held which job before becoming a judge?

    (A) Bailiff (B) Lawyer (C) Defendant (D) Stenographer

34. Gibbons v. Ogden is a dispute about _____ between _____.

    (A) Prices, Businesses (B) Trade, States (C) Transportation, States (D) Cars, People

35. A company ships its products with packing material that has a bad smell. This is:

    (A) A Tort (B) Slander (C) Marketing (D) A Poor Decision

36. In Texas v. Johnson the Supreme Court decided free speech includes _____.

    (A) Minors (B) Citizens (C) Court Documents (D) Symbols

37. The person hired to help the person accused of a crime is the:

    (A) Jury (B) Judge (C) Plaintiff Attorney (D) Defendant Attorney

38. A monopoly is illegal because it does not help a market have _____.

    (A) Customers (B) Competition (C) Contests (D) Computers

39. A right not given to the state or federal government is a right that belongs to the:

    (A) Courts (B) Citizens (C) President (D) Judges

40. A _____ is a judges decision used to better understand a future legal dispute.

    (A) Precedent (B) Statement (C) Complaint (D) Lien

YMBA Business Law Review Student Answer Sheet

Consider the questions on the previous four pages.
Write your answers in the spaces provided below.

1. _____   11. _____   21. _____   31. _____

2. _____   12. _____   22. _____   32. _____

3. _____   13. _____   23. _____   33. _____

4. _____   14. _____   24. _____   34. _____

5. _____   15. _____   25. _____   35. _____

6. _____   16. _____   26. _____   36. _____

7. _____   17. _____   27. _____   37. _____

8. _____   18. _____   28. _____   38. _____

9. _____   19. _____   29. _____   39. _____

10. _____ 20. _____   30. _____   40. _____

YMBA Business Law Drawing Board Answer Key

Page 9:

Page 11: laws created will vary, but each should have a positive result.
Page 13: (1) L (2) S (3) F (4) S (5) L (6) F (7) L (8) F
Page 15: country, law, judge, country, graduation cap
Page 17: (1) varies, but should be one of the first ten amendments (2) varies (3) answer should mention first amendment freedoms (4) varies (5) varies
Page 19: (1) E (2) C (3) L (4) G (5) I (6) F (7) A (8) J (9) M (10) B (11) H (12) D (13) K
Page 21: (1) verdict (2) court (3) room (4) guilty (5) defendant (6) person or party (7) trial (8) help (9) plaintiff (10) case (11) court
Page 23: summary of facts should include the details from page 22 and 23 to re-state the case. The decision should be to a refund to Jump Aroopo due to misrepresentation of the product in the catalog.
Page 24: if there was a true error or mistake there needs to be a way to correct the verdict for the innocent person. second question, opinion, answer will vary.
Page 25: circle: 1, 3, 7 cross out: 2, 4, 5, 6,
Page 27:

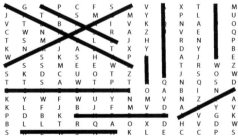

word scramble: evidence, lien, answer, expert, judgment

Page 29: (1) loan (2) gift (3) gift (4) loan (5) loan (6) slander (7) slander (8) libel (9) slander
Page 31: (1) up-goa-2018 (2) up-bus-2017 (3) up-cel-2018 (4) up-bun-2017 (5) pp-ave-2016 (6) pp-sta-2018 (7) cr-ban-2017 (8) cr-bha-2016 (9) up-dec-2018 (10) dp-ste-2018 (11) cr-tam-2016 (12) cr-bab-2018
Page 33: sparkle car wash, car dealer, january, december, sparkle car wash, services are to wash and clean cars, $7. additional contract details will vary.
Page 35: (1) illegal, minor so age too young to sign (2) legal (3) legal (4) illegal, minor so age too young to sign (5) illegal, minor so age too young to sign (6) legal (7) illegal, under doctor care and duress, during tooth removal (8) legal (9) legal (10) legal (11) will vary.
Page 37: (1) e (2) i (3) f (4) a (5) h (6) c (7) d (8) j (9) b (10) g
Page 39: $4,225.95, $4,675.95, $3,325.95, $5,575.95, $6925.95 (6) total damages: $24,729.75 (7) verdict varies, should have reasons for decision
Page 41: top row: tort, unethical, tort second row: tort (threat), tort, unethical third row: tort, unethical, unethical tic-tac-toe: diagonal across middle.
Page 43: (1) c (2) A (3) c and d (4) a and b (5) c (6) c (7) a and c (8) b
Page 45: (1) 2 (2) 6 (3) 1 (4) 4 (5) 8 (6) 3 (7) 9 (8) 5 (9) 7 (10) 10 (11) 11
Page 47: varies, but should include why the defendant is not guilty. second question varies, but should include why the defendant is guilty.
Page 49: (1) accept (2) accept (3) decline (4) decline (5) decline (6) decline (7) accept
Page 51: amendment 1 gives freedom and constitution gives freedom to pursue happiness. judges verdict agrees with plaintiff, southeast truck and transport company can use state roads to travel to another state as long as following roadway regulations.
Page 52: answer will vary, should have reasons to support the answer.
Page 53: amendment 1 is about freedom. unlike the 1922 supreme court case, Pizza Pal is not being excluded from the pizza industry by the defendants. The company is not being prevented from marketing to attract new customers. judges verdict: agree with defendant
Page 54: answer will vary, should have reasons to support the answer.
Page 55: amendment 6 = the right to a fair trial. the adult responsible for the minor child will be able to make decision in their interest. since the parents chose the attorney, and can afford the attorney, the court would not approve a tax payer attorney to represent the minor defendant. judges verdict = agree with defendant.
Page 56: answer will vary, should have reasons to support the answer.
Page 57: amendment 1 = freedom of speech. supreme court case tinker v. des moines supported the first amendment saying students are citizens and do not lose constitutional rights in a school building. judgment agrees with plaintiff, a minor under 18 years of age.
Page 58: answer will vary, should have reasons to support the answer.
Page 59: amendment 3 requires soldier to have homeowner permission to enter from this idea of real estate property rights can be the idea that homeowners choose to join the hoa community and in doing so have to agree with their rules to maintain the community atmosphere enjoyed by all homeowners the hoa creates rules. judges verdict agrees with the defendant, the HOA can make regulations regarding dogs.
Page 60: answer will vary, should have reasons to support the answer.
Page 61: amendment 1 covers free speech, free expression, free meetings of each citizen. students are citizen and how they choose to manage their own property when making a statement is a right granted in the constitution and supported by the supreme court verdict texas v. johnson.

Thank you for learning with YMBA.

Copyright Protected. 68 www.YMBAgroup.com

YMBA Business Law Review Answer Key

1. B
2. C
3. A
4. A
5. B
6. C
7. D
8. D
9. D
10. A

11. B
12. C
13. C
14. D
15. C
16. A
17. A
18. B
19. D
20. B

21. C
22. D
23. A
24. D
25. D
26. B
27. C
28. B
29. A
30. C

31. B
32. D
33. B
34. C
35. D
36. D
37. D
38. B
39. B
40. A

Certificate of Completion

Presented To

_____

Upon Successful Completion

of the

Youth Master of Business Administration

BUSINESS LAW

_____
Presented By

_____
Date

© www.YMBAgroup.com

SPLASH: A waterpark mystery

The champion is part of a secret plan! Solve the mystery as you meet Battle, twins Rachel and Reese, Zack and Morgan as they travel the United States with their parents. In this first book in the series the family begins a road trip adventure. The first *family fun stop* finds a mystery the family works together to solve. Join the family as they race to tell the judges. What was the secret plan? How will the kids find the judges to stop the results in time? What is discovered?
Grades 2-4/Ages 6-8/Early Chapter Book

Look Inside!

Chapter Books That Are Fun To Read and Include A Quiz To Demonstrate Completion

Skill Builder practice and a Book Quiz Included

Engaging Reading Books plus Skill Builders & a Book Quiz An easy way to demonstrate learning accomplishments.

57 Days Miriam Short Sails With William Penn

Join Miriam, Adam and Anne Mary, on their journey from England to America with William Penn to see the land he was granted in the New World by the King of England. Exciting history based on actual people and events. Experience the triumphs, struggles, loss and dreams while traveling across the Atlantic Ocean to a new home. Discover the path so many experienced as they left their home for America. Details vividly paint a picture of the conditions on the ship and the difficult days along the way. What challenges did they endure? What were the fears and hopes of the young adults? An exciting historical adventure of the journey to America. Join Miriam on her voyage with her family and William Penn.
GRADES 6-10/AGES 11-15/ FACTION CHAPTER BOOK

Available on AMAZON.com and retail sites such as BarnesandNoble.com

Y.M.B.A. Single Topic Learning Workbooks

Lesson Pages, Worksheets, A Quiz and A Certificate

Learn Life Skills & Business with Y.M.B.A.

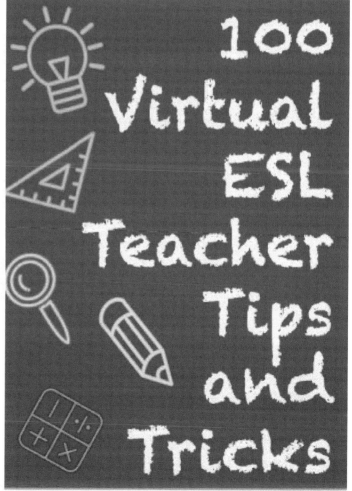

This one book can help you quickly achieve a successful virtual classroom.

100 Tips are ready to assist!

Recruiting for virtual teachers with a four year college degree, any major at: www.YMBAgroup.com

Printed by Amazon Italia Logistica S.r.l.
Torrazza Piemonte (TO), Italy